D1155319

CREATIVITY

The Key to a Remarkable Life

CONTENTS

01.

ABOUT THIS BOOK

02.

WHAT IS CREATIVITY?

03.

UNDERSTANDING CREATIVITY

04.

APPLYING CREATIVITY

05.

WHAT CREATIVITY IS NOT

06.

COMMUNICATING WITH CREATIVITY

07.

PROBLEM SOLVING WITH CREATIVITY

08.

CREATIVITY AND YOU

09.

YOU NEED CREATIVITY

10.

WHAT YOU NEED IN ORDER TO EMBRACE CREATIVITY

11.

MOVING FORWARD WITH CREATIVITY

ABOUT THIS BOOK

01.

WHY READ THIS BOOK?

Creativity can change your life.

You might think you're either a creative person or you're not. Many people think creativity is something that only some lucky people are born with, like a talent for painting, writing, composing music, or designing.

I want to show you that anyone can become a highly creative thinker, including you. I will show you how to use creativity to get what you want—whether that's happiness in your personal life or landing the job you crave or finding a solution to a problem.

You already are a creative human being. You just need to orient your mind toward creativity and open it up to think creatively. You must orient your thinking to newness—to come up with your own new ideas and be receptive to new ideas that others come up with.

We eat three times a day to nourish our bodies. We don't do as much to take care of our minds. Opening up your mind to creativity, using your imagination, expanding your horizons, seeing opportunities and options, and embracing a new way of thinking are like eating—they feed your mind.

The inspirational poet Maya Angelou said, "You can't use up creativity. The more you use, the more you have." [i]

Creativity can change your life if you open your mind.

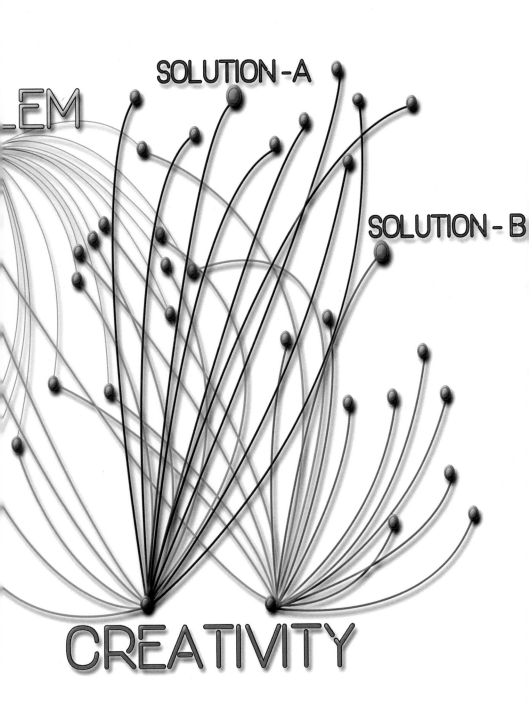

02.
WHY LISTEN TO ME?

That's my hero, Nobel laureate Desmond Tutu, supporting my work.

For the past 25 years, I've used creativity to influence hundreds of millions of people.

I have become renowned for using animation for social change in mass communications called behavior change communications. I've used animated short films to get people to think in a different way and come to their own conclusions to change their behavior.

My work focuses on creating innovative solutions to some of the world's toughest issues by effecting societal and individual behavioral change. I create human-centered communications across many cultures and countries to better the human condition.

I founded my company, Chocolate Moose Media, in Ottawa, Canada, in 1995 as a social enterprise. It consists of just one full-time person—me. I work alone from my house, using a team in several countries to create mass communications.

I have created, directed, and versioned, often on a volunteer basis, 4,300 animated behavior-change shorts in 50 series, covering a wide range of topics in human rights, diseases prevention, health, refugees, violence reduction, and nature. These shorts have been used in 198 countries, adapted to 400 language versions, and reached more than a billion people. I have won more than 110 awards, including some of the most prestigious.

My advice is based on creative thoughts that have changed the world.

My Vimeo channel contains 3,700 animated shorts for viewing, free download, and use. [ii]

This book is based on my work in creativity in the past 25 years. I've learned a lot in that period of time, and I'm happy to be passing my knowledge on to you.

03.
HOW TO USE THIS BOOK

This book is a very easy read, but it's meant to provoke thought, so don't rush through it. In fact, you could make it the slowest read you ever do!

There's no strict order to this book; it's not a story. You can be creative in how you read it. Feel free to randomly pick two or three pages and read just them.

If you want to be really creative about how you read this book, you can read it backwards—from the last point to the first! You'll get the same out of it as if you had read it in the traditional linear way.

Put this book down once in a while. Literally. Leave it and engage your mind. Then come back to it.

I give examples for most of the points I'm making. Sometimes I refer to my own work, and sometimes I use a historical reference. Think of your own examples in each case.

When I don't use an example, I make an assertion based on my many years immersed in creativity. Think about whether you agree or disagree with the assertion.

You may not agree with some, or even most, of my insights. That's fine. Disagreeing with a point is as valuable as agreeing with it.

At the end of each insight is a short takeaway. Reflect on each insight and takeaway before moving on. Think about how they might be applicable to you in your personal or professional life.

Let me be clear on what you won't learn. This book isn't going to teach you how to be a creative genius if you aren't one already. I can't make you into William Shakespeare or Thomas Edison or Coco Chanel.

When you've finished reading this book, keep it somewhere nearby. As you go on with your life after reading it, you might find that you want to come back to it from time to time. Make it your reference book on creativity.

This book is for you.

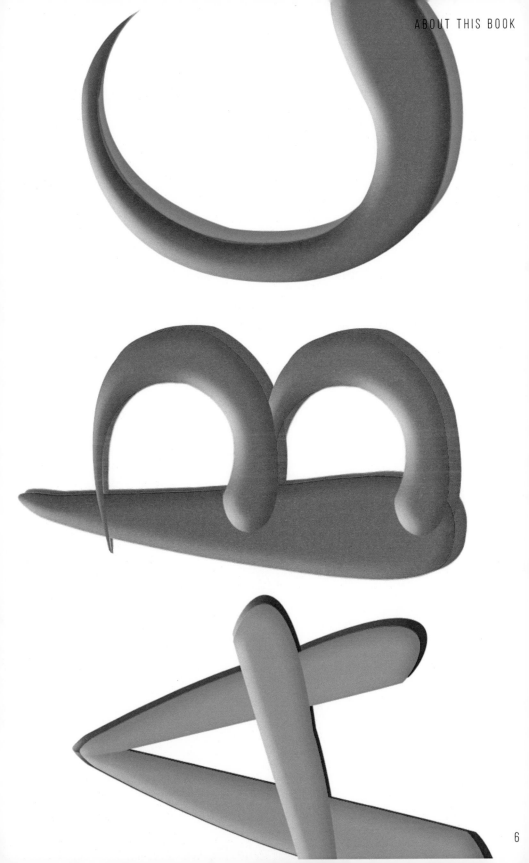

04.

THIS IS YOUR JOURNEY

Creativity is a personal journey of discovery.

You get to decide what you need to do to be the creative person you want to be and how creative a person you will be after you read this book. Read this book with your own mindset, understand and assess each point I make, and broaden your thinking as you progress through it.

Creativity is a mental balm for the soul. It's a process that engages and opens your mind. By reading through this book you'll gain a greater understanding of the whole of yourself.

Creativity is yours to discover.

WHAT IS CREATIVITY?

05.

CREATIVITY IS SIMPLE

Here is my simple definition in a single sentence:

Creativity is the ability to think differently via a mental process of original thoughts that leads to the creation of new ideas.

06.

CREATIVITY IS APPLICABLE EVERYWHERE

There is a huge misconception that creativity is limited to what is commonly called the arts: drawing, painting, sculpting, writing, composing, dancing, acting, designing, photographing, and filmmaking. All of these involve a big dose of creativity, but they are not the only applications. Creativity is not the same as artistry.

Mathematics seems to be the area most removed from creativity: there's nothing creative about an equation like one plus one equals two.

So, if you're a mathematician, do you think you don't need creativity? Of course, you do need it. Creativity cannot be applied in such a way that one plus one does not equal two, but it can be applied to the way mathematical problems are approached and solved. Creative thinking is often applied to lead to a formal proof in mathematics.

Creativity is especially useful in explaining complex scientific theories to non-scientists. Read the late physicist Stephen Hawking's books if you want superb evidence of this.

All the great scientific discoveries in the world have involved creativity, even if the discoveries were based in hard science. Creativity is in the mental process that leads to the discovery.

You don't have to change your job or activities to be a creative person. If even a mathematician needs creativity, so do you! It doesn't matter what you do. You can think creatively in any field of human endeavor.

Even if you're not involved in the arts, you can be creative.

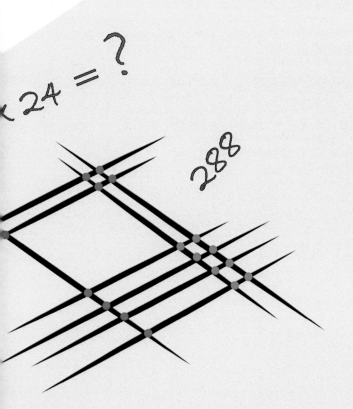

x 24 = ?

288

07.

CREATIVITY IS HAVING AN OPEN MIND

This is an image from a series I created on universal values for children. As you can see, the characters have, uh, "things" growing out of their heads. Why do they have these silly things? I'll tell you—there are no logical reasons. I added them because I think creatively.

Creativity is a transformational thought process. The best part of using creativity is that it makes you think in a much broader, more inclusive, and open-minded way.

A creative person sees, hears, feels, and thinks in a very different way than a narrow-minded, non-creative person. You will become more self-aware. You will discover yourself, and the world, from a new perspective.

My work in behavior change communications has shown me over and over that change cannot be imposed on a person. I have to get a viewer to watch my media, internalize the messaging, and then come to their own conclusion to change their behavior.

It's the same for you: you must decide for yourself that you want to be a creative thinker; I cannot impose creativity on you.

Decide for yourself right here and now that you want to expand your horizons. Make it a conscious choice. Without an explicit decision, you can't be a more creative person. Write down your intention if it helps.

Creativity opens your mind if you choose to let it.

iii

08.
CREATIVITY IS FUN

Albert Einstein apparently said, "Creativity is intelligence having fun." He was right. With creativity, you'll never be bored.

It doesn't matter what you do; thinking creatively is the fun part of life. Whether it's coming up with a new way to make your spouse laugh or doing something silly at work that brings you kudos, fun is an aspect of creative thinking that you'll be most satisfied with.

The majority of my work has been funny. Even though I deal with very serious subjects, I use humor to bring my audience to the serious point I'm making at the end of my films.

Humor has many advantages: it lowers the recipient's guard, gets their attention, increases their acceptance, and improves their retention.

Humor has an essential role in creative thinking. All humor has creativity.

**You'll have more fun in life as a
creative thinker.**

09.

CREATIVITY IS EXPRESSION

This is an image from an animation I directed centering on a powerful West African girl.

I have no formal education in producing or directing animation. I can't draw. I don't know how to manipulate software that creates animation. I cannot, in fact, create animation.

I direct animation by telling animators what I want and what I don't want. It works really well.

If you saw the movie Amadeus, based on the composer Wolfgang Amadeus Mozart, you might recall one of the last scenes in which Mozart is humming music and the composer, Salieri, is writing it down. My directing of animation is somewhat like that. It's the way I found to express myself creatively.

There is no single way to express creativity. Each of us expresses it in big and small ways by a huge variety of methods. You will find your own way based on your motivation and objectives.

You'll find a way to express your creativity.

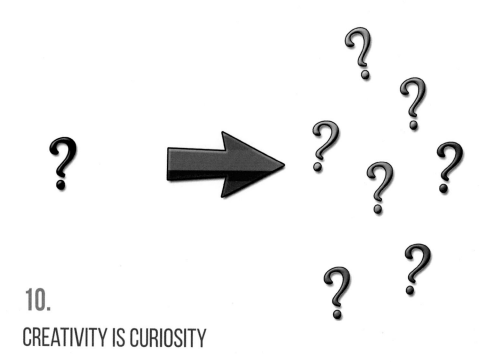

10.
CREATIVITY IS CURIOSITY

Creativity leads to many behaviors, but none is as closely related as curiosity. It is the curiosity in each of us that needs creativity.

What is the difference between creativity and curiosity? Curiosity leads us to ask one question; creativity leads us to ask multiple questions.

Creativity gives us the right questions to ask. What are all the reasons I can't communicate with my spouse? How can I change all the processes to engineer my product better? What are all the factors constraining my company from doing better?

Get your mind thinking about all the possible questions. Question everything!

Be curious and ask many questions.

11.

CREATIVITY IS ALL AROUND YOU

Put down this book for a minute and look around you.

Look at your clothes. Look at your shoes. Look at your watch. Look at your mobile phone. Look at your computer. Look at whatever is opposite you. Look to the left; now look to the right. If you're sitting, stand up and look at your chair.

Whatever you see has resulted from creative thinking. It came out of someone's brain. It was designed. It was produced as an outcome of creative thinking.

Everything made by humans involves creativity. There isn't a single item that didn't involve creativity, even if the product is highly technical, such as your computer or mobile phone. Actually, the more technical a product is, the more creativity was required to create it.

Widen your perception to see creativity everywhere you look.

12.
CREATIVITY IS WHAT GRABS YOU

This is one of the most famous chairs in the world. The Dutch designer and architect Gerrit Rietveld created it in 1918. Rietveld himself seems to have viewed his chair as a work of art, as he called it a "spatial" creation: a sculpture in space rather than a piece of furniture.

Not even art and design students know this chair as it was in its original state. It wasn't until 1923, when the chair was painted, that it became famous. Painting it in bold colors was a simple creative decision that started Rietveld's long-lasting impact on the world of design and architecture.

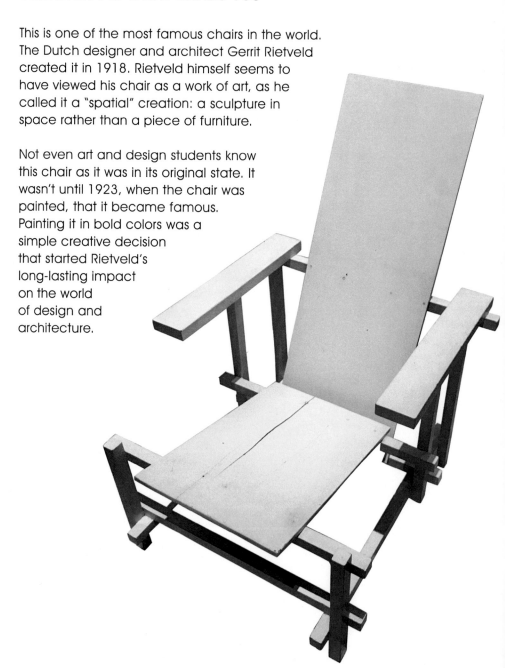

Here's what it looks like in the design books today:

This is the chair I'm with on the cover. I have one of these chairs in my apartment. I love it, even though my guests are all frustrated because I ask them not to sit in it!

Never buy a bland gray suit or a plain beige dress again. Creativity is the opposite of dullness.

Look for what grabs you.

13.

CREATIVITY IS BEING DIFFERENT

Like every watch, this watch tells the time. But this watch tells the time differently than your average watch. It doesn't use two hands to tell time. The hour is the large white number you see. The second hand indicates the date.

It's from the mind of Gerald Genta, a Swiss creative genius regarded as the greatest watch designer who ever lived. If you know anything about watchmaking, you know about Gerald Genta.

Seek the different. Be the Gerald Genta of your industry. Creativity makes the mundane magical.

Be different.

14.
CREATIVITY IS THE UNUSUAL

This is a bookcase or room divider. It might not be to your taste, but it is a result of great creative thinking.

An Italian architect and designer named Ettore Sottsass designed it. He formed a group of designers called the Memphis Group. What did it have to do with Memphis, Tennessee? Nothing. The name came from a song playing in the background at the group's inaugural meeting. The name itself was creative.

Creativity is the opposite of normalcy.

My apartment is filled with unusual items. It's got Alice-in-Wonderland-style furniture and very colorful paintings. The bookcase pictured would fit right in because I surround myself with creatively designed decor.

You don't have to go to the extreme of filling your house with unusual or colorful items; your surroundings should reflect your taste and make you feel comfortable. But try looking at everyday things and furniture you buy and think creatively. Once in a while, buy an item that looks like it resulted from creative thinking.

Reach for the unusual.

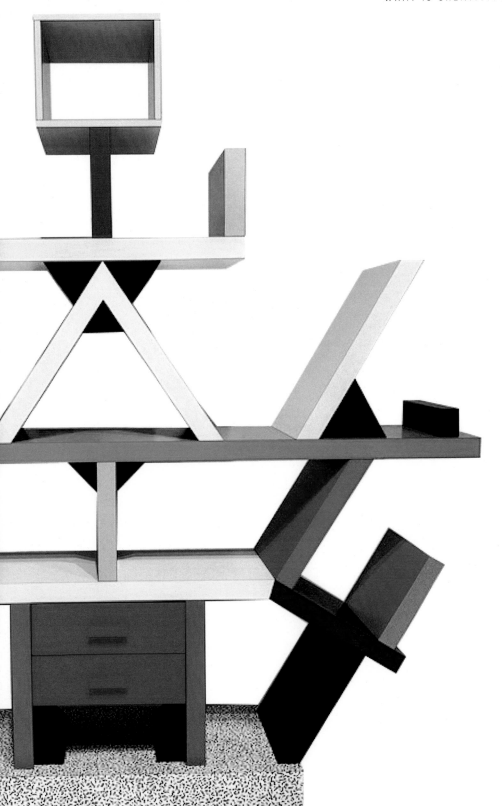

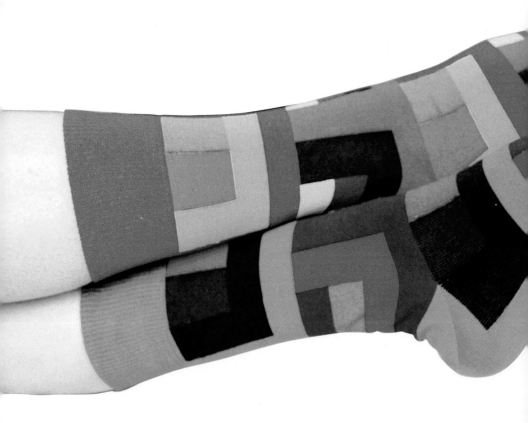

15.

CREATIVITY IS ADOPTING WILD IDEAS

What's the wildest idea you've ever had? Wild ideas result from creative thinking.

Have you ever deliberately worn two different socks? Try it. You might find it liberating. It's a wild idea that won't hurt anyone or cost much if you implement it, and it might just open your mind to thinking creatively. And if someone else notices you are wearing two different socks, you'll draw him or her into thinking creatively, too.

What's a wild idea to you? Think of some ideas. Write them down. Pick out the ones you want to try.

Embrace wild ideas.

16.

CREATIVITY IS WHAT MAKES THE IMPOSSIBLE POSSIBLE

I was commissioned by the Arabic-speaking Al Jazeera Children's Channel to create a series on values for children. I directed a series on values such as gender equality, racism, accepting other cultures, and other issues.

Many mass communicators would have balked at this commission. I embraced it. It was the biggest challenge I'd ever faced. I knew that creativity would be the most important element.

I had a lot of decisions to make. Should boys and girls be at the same school? Yes. Would they sit at the same desk? No. Should women have their heads covered? Definitely the elderly.

You can imagine that this was an assignment fraught with peril. Surely, beaming an animated series in Arabic directly into the living rooms of more than 50 million households in 30 countries for two years, with 46 short films on issues such as equality between boys and girls or racism prevention, could have provoked a huge backlash.

It didn't.

While writing and designing and animating the series, I paid very close attention to every element of the communications my team was creating, to every word in the scripts, and to every image we were drawing. Creativity was used in a way that got clear messages across without creating a storm.

What seems impossible at first glance usually isn't. With creativity, nothing is impossible.

The key is to use your creativity to its utmost. Indeed, this is the only way to do the impossible.

Do the impossible.

UNDERSTANDING CREATIVITY

17.

CREATIVITY IS DOING

When you look around you and see objects designed and produced as a result of creative thinking, you see the results of "doing." You can have the most brilliant and creative thought in your head, but if you don't do something with it, it's of no use to anyone, including yourself.

How would we see in the dark if Thomas Edison hadn't persisted until he created the modern light bulb? What if the Wright brothers had only dreamed of flying instead of using their creativity to create an airplane? Where would we be if Tim Berners-Lee hadn't done something about his ideas on information management and created the modern Internet?

Each of them followed through with actions; they did. You must do.

Follow a creative thought with a related action.

18.
CREATIVITY REQUIRES DAYDREAMING

Ever been bored? Uninterested?

There's no standard psychological definition of boredom. We know when we feel bored, but each of us has a different threshold of lack of stimulation that causes boredom.

What do most people do when they are bored? They daydream. They let their minds wander away from their surroundings. They go away for a while, and then they come back to the present.

For many people, daydreaming is a meaningless activity having no impact or a negative impact. But daydreaming can also have a positive impact.

Daydreaming is a critical component of creative thinking. Because daydreaming is a thought process that takes you away from what is demanding your attention, it can lead to highly creative ideas and problem solving since you have an open mind that is not connected to stimuli happening in front of you.

The next time you're bored, no matter what the setting, let your mind wander but think creatively. Channel your daydreaming into thinking of new ideas. Think of a problem, then think of a solution. You have a better chance of thinking of a solution precisely because you're not paying attention to what is happening around you.

With apologies to teachers everywhere, I suggest that you intentionally engage in daydreaming once in a while. Don't always stay focused on the present stimuli; let your mind wander.

Be a daydreamer.

iv

19.
CREATIVITY LASTS AND LASTS

Ludwig van Beethoven said he wanted his music to change the world. He was clear about the impact he wanted to make.

He succeeded. He used his creative thinking to write music that we listen to today, some 200 years after he wrote it. His famous nine symphonies live on, and you can also hear a modern recording of the first known composition he wrote when he was just 12 years old.

He was initially just a boy with a dream. When he wrote his first note, he did not know the huge reach through the ages that it would have. Great creativity doesn't die.

Create something long-lasting.

20.

CREATIVITY MEANS AN ATTRACTION TO COMPLEXITY

At times in my professional life, I have had the good fortune of being able to turn down projects because they were too easy. I like the most difficult challenges. Stopping sexual assault, preventing a deadly infectious disease, and promoting universal values are examples of issues I've loved working on.

Some of the most creative people are computer programmers. That's because all software coding is new. Software coding is usually necessary to solve complex problems. Most modern jet aircraft, highly complex machines, are flown longer in a flight using autopilot software, rather than by humans.

Creative thinkers are often attracted to the difficult or complex. This doesn't mean creativity cannot be applied to the easy. However, the more complex the problem, the more that creativity is needed.

Reach for the complex.

21.

CREATIVITY IS BEING CONCISE

This is an image from a short I created to convey the message that asbestos kills. The girl says a tiny fiber killed her father. My script was just a few words and the whole video is just 30 seconds long.

It's a difficult task to get a coherent message out in a short length of time. This is especially true in languages with words of varying lengths. The more space or time you have to deliver a message, the less creative you must be. Creativity is brevity.

Here are some of the short, concise, clear taglines I've used in my work:
- Use a condom; stop the spread of AIDS
- Don't wait—vaccinate
- Mosquitoes cause malaria

Try it. Think of a long message. Now say it aloud in no fewer than five sentences. Stop. Think about the message again. Now deliver it aloud in no more than five words. Which one required more creativity?

Be brief and to the point.

22.

CREATIVITY LEADS TO LIFELONG LEARNING

I have nine degrees and certificates from eight universities in Canada, the United States, and the United Kingdom. It's not "too much." In fact, it's not enough. I want to learn more.

Creativity leads to the feeling that you're always learning. Whether it's in or outside of the classroom, a creative mind is always seeking knowledge. It's what drives creativity.

Is there something you would like to learn but haven't yet? Start now. Take a course. Read a book or an article. Talk to an expert. Watch a lecture online. Do anything that gives you information.

Promise yourself to never stop learning. Seek and absorb knowledge. It's part of the process of expanding your mind and being a creative thinker.

Start a continual learning process today.

23.

CREATIVITY CAN HELP YOU DECIDE WHICH HABITS TO KEEP

We all have habits.

Think of what you do at the beginning of each day. You get up at roughly the same time. You go through the same morning ritual, such as brushing your teeth, taking a shower, getting dressed, getting coffee or tea, and going to work.

One of my heroes is Charles Schultz, the creator of the Peanuts comic strips and animations. I believe he did more for animation than anyone, with the possible exception of Walt Disney (I don't want every animator who reads this to faint because they all worship him!).

I love the Peanuts characters. Snoopy is my favorite.

Schultz was a creature of habit. For example, he ate the same food at the same table in his restaurant, the Warm Puppy Café, almost every day.

How could a person of such repetition be so creative? He was very creative in his work, so he did not need to apply his creative mind in other areas. He stayed with what was comfortable in the real world and allowed his creative thinking to create the imaginary world of Peanuts.

Thinking creatively does not mean you must be creative in every sphere of your world. It does not mean you have to abandon all your habits and suddenly look for the new. However, if you do want to change your habits, creativity gives you the wherewithal to do so.

Change your unwanted habits.

24.

CREATIVITY CAN MAKE YOU A LOT OF MONEY

Everyone who ever founded a company, no matter how big or small, used creativity.

Think of all the largest companies in the world today. At the end of 2019, the seven largest publicly traded companies by market capital were (in order from biggest): [v]

1. Apple, founded by Steve Jobs and Steve Wozniak
2. Microsoft, founded by Bill Gates and Paul Allen
3. Alphabet (Google), founded by Larry Page and Sergey Brin
4. Amazon, founded by Jeff Bezos
5. Facebook, founded by Mark Zuckerberg
6. Alibaba, founded by Jack Ma
7. Berkshire Hathaway, founded by Warren Buffett

One or two creative individuals founded each of the world's largest companies.

These companies aren't huge because they're exploiting the Earth's minerals or in traditional industries like transportation or making the most widgets; they're huge because of the ideas of one or two people. That's why the founders are famous.

Creativity is what every self-made person has used to get rich.

**If you want to be rich, you need
to think creatively.**

25.

CREATIVITY IS THINKING BIG

That's a George Foster Peabody Award. It's given for "stories that matter."
It's the most prestigious award in my field. It was given to me because of a
series I directed that made a difference.

When you think creatively, you will realize that you can make a difference. It
comes as a corollary to thinking creatively.

You might make a difference in your own life or in your family or company
or community, or in the world at large.

Think it can't be done? Think of your own hero. Think about why that person
is your hero. It's probably because he or she made a difference—perhaps
to the world at large or perhaps just to you.

Just realizing you can make a difference and then starting to make a
difference is thinking big. You can do it.

**Creativity will make you realize that you
can make a difference.**

26.

CREATIVITY CAN SAVE LIVES

More than 400,000 people die of malaria every year.

This is the Buzz and Bite malaria prevention campaign I created. This campaign, consisting of two funny animated female anopheles mosquitos that are out to infect the world with malaria, has been used in more than half of the countries that have malaria. It consists of 30 animated short videos and is currently in 39 languages.

The campaign is typical of my work: animated, humorous, multilingual, distributed widely, and free to the world.

Can you imagine a malaria prevention campaign without creativity? It is creative thinking that enables this kind of work to be done. This work saves lives.

Save lives with creativity.

APPLYING CREATIVITY

27.

YOU HAVE APPLIED YOUR CREATIVITY ALREADY

My company is called Chocolate Moose Media. That's a creative name, huh?

Why Chocolate Moose? Well, because I love chocolate. I might even be a closet chocoholic! The moose (the animal, not the dessert) is the Canadian part.

Very few people can remember my name, Firdaus Kharas. I admit it is rather unusual and a difficult name for many people to pronounce. So, I needed a memorable name for my company: one that denotes creativity.

You have already applied creativity in many different ways throughout your life. Stop and think about what they are. If you can think of many ways, make a list.

What's your pet's name (or, if you don't have a pet, your friend's pet's name)? I'm sure that's a creative name! Now recall how you named the pet. That was you thinking creatively and then expressing your creativity in a name.

You've already applied your creativity many, many times.

28.

CREATIVITY IS NOT UNLIMITED TALENT

Can you do this?

This is the Gallery of Maps, and it leads to the incomparable Sistine Chapel in the Vatican.

If I gave you a blank corridor and some paint, do you think you could create that? You're probably thinking "No way!" Let's move on, then, because you know there are limits to your ability to paint.

There are limits to your talents even if you become a highly creative thinker.

You don't have unlimited talent.

29.

CREATIVITY MEANS ACCEPTING THAT YOU HAVE LIMITS

All right, how about this?

This painting is a self-portrait by Rembrandt.

If I gave you a canvas and some paint, could you create this? "Probably not," you say? Fine, let's accept that, as this is a remarkable and very difficult painting.

Accept that you can't do everything creative.

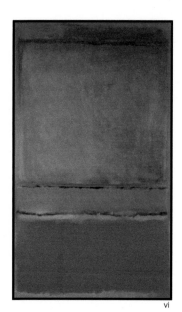

vi

30.

CREATIVITY IS BROADENING YOUR LIMITS

Can you paint something like this?

If you can, stop reading this book immediately and start painting! It's a brilliant painting by Mark Rothko, and it reportedly sold for €140 million (about $186 million) in 2014.

Even if you've never painted, consider whether you could do it if you wanted to. Maybe you could create a similar painting if you tried. Perhaps your limits aren't as narrow as you think they are.

Maybe you can do more than you think you can.

31.

CREATIVITY IS AUTHENTICITY

Here's an easy one. Can you do this?

Yes, it's a blank canvas on a wall. You can do that, right? Nothing to it!

If I showed you this photo and gave you this exact canvas and showed you precisely where to hang it, would you think you're being creative?

Sorry, but that wouldn't make you creative. You'd be copying, not being creative.

Creativity must have authenticity. You need a genuinely new idea, even if it's easy.

Don't copy.

32.

CREATIVITY MEANS NOT HAVING TO WAIT FOR "EUREKA!"

With creativity, you don't have to wait for a sudden big thought. You don't have to continually search for "the next big thing."

We've all experienced small moments of abrupt realization—when something that didn't make sense suddenly does. We have these minor epiphany moments many times in life, particularly when we are learning. Suddenly, what we're learning makes sense.

Creativity is a continual thought process. Even the most creative people in the world might never have a single big, important "Aha!" moment. Instead, creative thinkers have series of ideas, and they come to realizations one after the other.

Don't wait for Eureka!

33.
CREATIVITY REQUIRES PERSISTENCE

Creativity is not a one-off method of thinking; it requires persistence. Persistence is doggedly pursuing something.

I'm not very good at tying my shoelaces. Honestly. No matter how tightly I tie them, they always seem to come loose.

What does creativity have to do with me tying my shoelaces? It's central to my thinking because I'm trying to find the best way to get them to stay tied. I try all sorts of creative lacings and knots. I admit that some of them look sillier than others.

vii

Try tying your shoelaces a different way the next time you put your shoes on. And then, the next time, try another way. And then try yet another. You have a lot of choices. Mathematically, there are at least a million ways you could lace and tie your shoelaces. I'm very slowly going through each one!

A non-creative thinker will come up with perhaps five ways of tying shoelaces; a creative thinker will figure out at least 50. How many ways can you think of to tie your shoelaces?

Be persistent.

34.

CREATIVITY CAN LEAD TO UNEXPECTED DISCOVERIES

You may be trying to create something new. In the process of trying, you could accidentally create something else.

History is full of great advances that were discovered accidentally. Many of these have saved countless lives. Penicillin and X-rays are two such discoveries.

Here's an example that doesn't involve high science: Velcro.

In 1941, a Swiss engineer named George de Mestral went for a hike in the Alps with his dog. Upon returning home, he noticed that small burdock burrs (seeds) had stuck to his clothes. He saw that the seeds were covered in very small hooks, which is how they became attached to the fabric. From that observation, he created the material we now call Velcro. It took him 14 years to perfect and patent Velcro.

For many generations before 1941, burrs stuck to people's clothes. Yet no one had thought of creating a useful application based on the concept.

It was de Mestral's creative mind that made the difference. When he came back from that walk, he thought creatively.

You might have unexpected success.

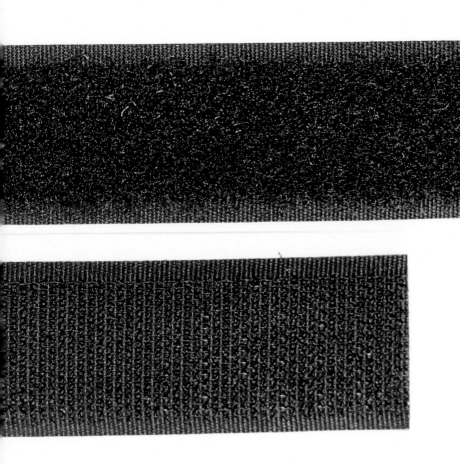

35.

CREATIVITY IS HUMAN-CENTERED

This is a Reliant Robin, which, you'll notice, has just one front wheel. It was sold in the United Kingdom for 30 years.

Someone used their creativity to design this car. Certainly, it was unusual. It was also inherently unstable and put drivers and passengers at risk.

Think about that: a badly designed car with three wheels was funded, manufactured, distributed, reviewed, sold, bought, and driven for 30 years. And all this time, almost every other model of car on the planet had four wheels!

I've seen a lot of creative ideas implemented as if it they were for aliens. The designers who've created products that don't work had one thing in common: they didn't make the audience they were designing for their only priority.

Good creative thinking is about implementing ideas that create processes and products that are feasible, practical, functional, accessible, and useful. Creativity does not always mean automatic success.

Think about various annoyances you've encountered, from something as simple as packaging that was very difficult to open to incomprehensible instructions in a product manual to slow service at a restaurant that could be sped up. The list is endless.

Time and time again, governments, companies, and individuals forget whom they are being creative for: people.

Humans must be central to your thinking.

36.

CREATIVITY IS TRUSTING YOURSELF

This is an image from an animated video I created to explain what the COVID-19 virus is, how to protect yourself from getting infected, and what to do if you are infected.

Look at that face. What do you get out of it?

The message I used with that image was "Do not panic," just three words. Stark. Unambiguous. Blunt. Direct.

I wrote "Do not panic" into the script because I felt that the world was treating the virus as if it were a guillotine. It was as if getting infected meant an automatic death sentence. In fact, for most people everywhere, the chances of survival far exceeded the chances of dying.

I could not have written those three words as a command if I wasn't absolutely convinced of the value of what I was doing.

Have confidence in the validity of your ideas.

viii

37.
CREATIVITY IS A SOLITARY PURSUIT

Creativity is what you have in your mind. It has nothing to do with anyone else. Your creativity is yours alone.

Charles Schultz was an extremely creative person. He worked alone. He drew every one of his 17,987 comic strips by himself.

You're going to be on a singular journey if you want to be a creative person. It should start now and last the rest of your life. Get going!

**Don't be afraid of a solitary
journey into creativity.**

WHAT CREATIVITY IS NOT

ix

38.

CREATIVITY IS NOT A PRODUCT

This is a sheet of music by Wolfgang Amadeus Mozart. His "product" was simply ink on a piece of paper.

Mozart was, undoubtably, a great creative thinker. But his creative genius wasn't visual—it was the thought process that led him to write such beautiful music.

Think of it this way: anyone who knows music can scratch notes on paper. Anyone can create the same product as Mozart.

Mozart is an excellent example of creative thinking because he fully composed the music in his brain before he wrote it down. He never went through drafts of compositions.

Products are the result of creative thinking. Products show you what creativity creates.

Don't look at your tangible end product and think "That's creativity!"

39.

CREATIVITY IS NOT INNOVATION

Innovation is the new buzzword; everybody wants it. You might have noticed that innovation is not what I'm writing about. Why is that?

Innovation is the result of creative thinking. Innovation is the result of implementing creativity.

Innovation can't happen without creativity. To be innovative, you must be a creative person.

Many "gurus" tell companies and individuals how to be innovative. Some of them are useless. When their advice doesn't work out, it's usually because they haven't understood what needs to happen before innovation: creativity, the mental process that leads to innovation.

Innovation is not a starting point. It's one possible outcome of creative thinking.

Creative thinking comes before innovation.

40.

CREATIVITY IS NOT STAGNATION

While innovation is the result of creative thinking, we still need it. In fact, we need much more of it than is happening now.

Innovation is what moves the world forward: sometimes in small incremental steps, sometimes in a giant leap.

Problems, ranging from large ones such as global pollution to small ones such as how you'll find your lost keys, all require innovation.

It's essential to have innovation or nothing would progress. That's how companies, communities, countries, and even the whole planet evolve. So, we must have lots of creative thinking that results in lots of innovation.

The future of the planet depends on creativity.

41.

CREATIVITY IS NOT LOGICAL THINKING

The brain is divided into two hemispheres. Scientists disagree on whether one side can be dominant over the other, but they do know that different parts of the brain control different types of thinking.

Analysis is associated with logical thinking, which is thought to be in the left brain. This fishbone chart is one example of an analytical tool.

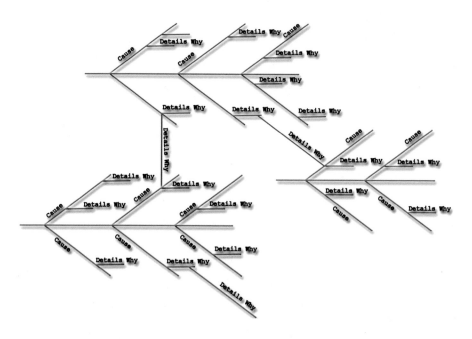

Doing analysis by following this diagram may be very useful in other processes, but it isn't good for creativity. This type of diagram could lead to a killer of creativity: overanalysis.

Creativity relies on a different kind of thinking: right-brain thinking. Closely associated to creative thinking are other right-brain thinking processes, especially imagination and intuition.

Unleash your imagination and intuition.

42.
CREATIVITY IS NOT FOCUS GROUPS [x]

This is Steve Jobs, the co-founder of Apple. He said:

"It's really hard to design products by focus groups. A lot of times, people don't know what they want until you show it to them." [xi]

You know how successful Apple, a company built on creativity, has become. Be like Steve Jobs.

Traditional business schools are focused on techniques for creating and selling products or services. But focus groups, usability testing, product testing, and feedback loops are killers of creativity.

When thinking creatively, avoid focus groups.

43.

CREATIVITY IS NOT BRAINSTORMING

Adrian Furnham is an author of 90 books. He works at the Business Psychology Unit at University College, London. He has concluded:

Research shows unequivocally that brainstorming groups produce fewer and poorer quality ideas than the same number of individuals working alone. Yet firms continue to use brainstorming as a technique for generating ideas. [xiii]

I believe brainstorming groups have an appropriate part to play in generating creative ideas, but they should not be the starting point. The best creative ideas come from individuals, although groups may contribute to idea evolution, such as by helping determine implementation.

This observation is based on where creative ideas originate. Each of us has our own creative ideas. Creative ideas coming out of a group process are the synthesis of one or more individual's ideas. Step one: Think for yourself. Step two: Share your thoughts.

Two important components of creative thinking are the use of imagination and intuition. Groups cannot, by definition, have imagination or intuition; only individuals can.

Picture the most creative person you can think of. Who is it? For me, it's Leonardo da Vinci. He was an unparalleled creative genius. If da Vinci had belonged to a group through which he funneled his ideas, we probably wouldn't know his name today.

Can you name any group that came up with history-changing ideas? I can't. But I can name many highly creative individuals.

xii I do most of my creative thinking alone in the shower—which sometimes results in unusually long showers! Where do you do your best creative thinking?

The best creative ideas come from individuals.

44.

CREATIVITY IS NOT GROUPTHINK

Groups are inherently uncreative.

I hate big groups, especially at the beginning stages of problem solving. The larger the group, the less creative the results.

Groups often create lowest-common-denominator results. That's because each person in a group brings their own set of ideas, experiences, and perceptions. When you put them all together, you don't get creativity; you get groupthink.

Groupthink happens when people lose their independence. The group members come to a decision or conclusion because they want to conform or harmonize or be cohesive. Conflict is avoided, alternatives are not explored, and critical thinking goes out the window.

Creativity doesn't stand a chance in such an environment.

Never use a group as a starting point for creativity.

45.
CREATIVITY IS NOT DICTATORSHIP

Have you ever been:

- At a meeting in which everyone just nodded their heads at what the leader said?
- At a presentation in which the speaker asked for questions but really wanted none?
- Given advice to "Just get on board" or "Go with the flow"?
- Told to not be "different" or "difficult"?

Dictatorship can come in many guises. Sometimes it can be subtle and sometimes it can be overt. It can be severe or mild.

Dictators express themselves in a variety of ways, from issuing outright orders and demands to putting people down and insulting them. They rush to judgment. They love to control. They like employing sarcasm and skepticism. They are insidious and treacherous.

Dictators are everywhere. They can be your spouse or your parent or your boss or your colleague or your teacher.

Dictators have no creativity in themselves and are dreaded killers of creativity in others. They reach their own conclusions quickly. They don't want to hear, consider, or do anything that they haven't thought of. They certainly don't want to implement your creative ideas.

Never be, or give in to, a dictator.

46.

CREATIVITY IS NOT LONELINESS

W. S. Gilbert and Arthur Sullivan were highly creative people who collaborated to create 14 comic operas. Each of them had a unique contribution: Gilbert wrote the words and Sullivan composed the music.

I have co-created several media series with the imaginative South African producer and writer Brent Quinn.

xiv

xiv

Sometimes two or more creative people can work together to create something new. Creativity does not mean creative thinkers cannot collaborate to pool their thinking and create something that is not possible for one person to create alone.

There are two keys to success. First, whomever you collaborate with must also be creative; ideally, at least as creative as you. Second, each of you is working on a different aspect of creating something in the spirit of collaboration.

You don't always have to work alone.

47.

CREATIVITY IS NOT POSSIBLE WITH MANY OTHERS LOOKING OVER YOUR SHOULDER

When I produce media, the worst experience I have is when I encounter what I call "Creating by Committee Syndrome." It's when the organization or company I'm working for has a committee to oversee the work I'm doing.

This problem is at its worst when the committee members all feel that they must exercise control because they're the "experts." They're usually experts in their fields, such as doctors who are trained in medicine, yet they believe they have the expertise to direct mass communications. I've walked away from some projects because of Creating by Committee Syndrome.

In filmmaking, the area I work in, there's only one person in charge of the creative side of the project. He or she is called the director. You see that person's vision in a film or video. That person should be left alone to create.

Keep an open mind but push back on being forced to change your creative ideas.

48.

CREATIVITY IS NOT HAVING A CRYSTAL BALL

This is the evolution of the mobile telephone. Someone used the full power of their creative mind to design each of these models, which were each state of the art at the time.

The person who designed the first model couldn't, at that time, design the second, and so on.

xv

Creativity is not the ability to see the future. Creativity leads to new ideas that produce innovations, but the innovations are grounded in what is possible at the time. Creativity happens within a context.

**Use your creative
abilities as they exist
now.**

49.

CREATIVITY IS NOT THE OBVIOUS

I saw this display at my local coffee shop. I have no idea why someone thought there needed to be a sign next to the bananas stating the obvious, but there it was.

The obvious is the opposite of creativity. Something that is what it is needs no creativity.

Never state the obvious, because the obvious doesn't need to be stated. That's obvious!

The obvious has nothing to do with creativity.

50.

CREATIVITY IS NOT BEING DIFFERENT FOR ITS OWN SAKE

I laugh at communications that aren't clear. Sometimes they're very creative! This is a sign I saw at a hotel in Texas. I'm still scratching my head, trying to figure it out.

It's definitely different. I've stayed at thousands of hotels in the 146 countries I've traveled to, and I've never seen another sign stating the check-in time before the check-out time.

Creativity must make sense. Pressing harder on a remote control when the batteries are dead isn't being creative, it's being lazy. Speaking louder when someone doesn't understand you is not creativity, it's being boneheaded.

**Creativity is not just
being different; it must
make sense.**

51.

CREATIVITY IS NOT MEASURABLE

This is a painting by Vincent van Gogh. Today he's regarded as a creative genius, and his paintings sell for tens of millions of dollars. Yet, during his lifetime, almost no one bought his paintings. Historians tell us that he sold very few of them and that he probably bartered many for food and lodging.

If the bean counters of today had evaluated Van Gogh's success during his lifetime, they would have concluded that he was an abject failure. After all, his goal was to sell his paintings.

You and I now look at his paintings far more favorably than his contemporaries did, but that doesn't change the fact that he was a creative genius when he painted the paintings, even if no one recognized it at the time.

I've been asked to create a behavior change video, show it to masses of people, and then evaluate the results, proving that it changed people's behavior, all in a span of three months. I've never accepted those assignments.

Don't fall into the evaluation trap! In the immortal words of Tony Soprano, "Forget about it."

Don't focus on others' judgments of what constitutes success.

52.

CREATIVITY IS NOT RISK-FREE

If you're:

- Cautious
- Timid
- Risk-averse
- Conservative
- Not willing to be wrong
- Afraid of failure

you're not going to be a creative person. Failure is very much a part of the creative process. It also helps you move on quickly because it's creativity that will help you see the next success.

Risk-taking is inherently part of creative thinking. After all, new ideas involve some degree of risk because they haven't been tried.

When you do fail, move on quickly. We only tend to do that when physical activity is involved: if we are learning to skate, we fall and get up and try again very quickly.

We're less likely to move on quickly when we think that failure displays our weakness, especially in our work environment. We worry about what others think and so we don't try again, lest we fail again.

Some of the world's greatest experts on failure are research scientists. They experiment all the time. They know right from the start that their experiment will probably fail. In fact, some say 90 percent of scientific experiments fail.

Yet research scientists persist. They fail, and they fail, and they fail, until they don't. Breakthroughs happen because they try again. The world is vastly better off because of their tenacity and courage.

You need to not be afraid of failing. Own your failures. Prepare yourself mentally to fail. Tell yourself it's OK to fail.

Fail. And then use creativity to find your next success.

53.

CREATIVITY IS NOT HITTING YOUR HEAD AGAINST A BRICK WALL

If you fail, you don't need to hit your head against a brick wall.

One of the most difficult decisions we all must make is when to change course. Think about your life. You may know something isn't quite right, but you don't know what it is.

- Are you studying a subject you're not really into?
- Do you feel trapped in a job you don't like but think you have no choice because you need a paycheck?
- Have you not taken a vacation in years because you're "too busy"?

These are examples of big brick walls. Some walls are much smaller but still right there. Sometimes they're visible, but sometimes they're not.

When you can't see an obstacle in front of you, you need to be a creative thinker. The more creative you are, the more likely you will be to see an invisible wall.

Creativity can help you see your walls and options for changing course.

Creative thinking means seeing what can't be easily seen.

54.

CREATIVITY IS NOT BEING A TORTOISE

You probably know of Aesop's fable of The Tortoise and the Hare. I directed a variation of the fable in animation in Africa's first-ever animated series.

In a nutshell, the hare moves much faster than the tortoise. However, the hare is sleepy and takes a nap during the race. The slow and steady tortoise, following a straight path to the finish, wins the race.

In the modern world, slow and steady doesn't win the race. The creative thinker wins the race!

I envision the hare winning because he set an alarm on his smartphone, took the nap he wanted, got up on time, slapped on his roller skates, and zipped to the finish line before the plodding tortoise. There he is, using creativity to reach all of his objectives.

Win your races. Use creativity to reach all your objectives.

COMMUNICATING WITH CREATIVITY

55.

YOU NEED TO COMMUNICATE

Creativity and communication are inextricably linked. Creativity is a key to effective communication and communication is a key to creative thinking.

Think of boring communication you've heard or seen. It could be a mind-numbing lecture by a professor or a movie with no plot that put you to sleep.

Now think of stimulating communication you've heard or seen. The difference between the boring and the stimulating is creativity.

Because creative thinking involves new ideas, you must get people to think, see, hear, feel, or act in a new way. You must communicate well in order to get your audience to understand and accept what is new. That's not an easy task because people are comfortable with the status quo—with what they already know or do.

There are many ways of formulating and communicating thoughts, such as reasoning, having a logical argument, and exchanging information. Of the many ways of communicating ideas, persuasion is the one that most needs creative thinking.

You need to use creativity especially when you're trying to change someone's attitudes, intentions, motivations, beliefs, or behavior. The more creativity you use, the more likely you are to succeed.

**Use creativity to reach your
audience.**

56.

UNDERSTANDING YOUR AUDIENCE IS NOT EASY

Barriers to communications are what separate and distinguish human beings. A barrier can be emanating from, or directed against, a person. Every human being has a multitude of barriers to communication that create a mindset.

First, you need to know what the barriers are. Second, you need to grasp each of them. Third, you must design around these barriers. Creativity comes to the fore in the designing part.

In my work in mass communications in the past 25 years, I've had to profoundly understand my audiences because the work involved reaching hundreds of millions of people in almost every country, in dozens of languages, across numerous barriers such as cultural and religious beliefs. I've had to carefully design around barriers to reach people. That involved a lot of creativity.

Profoundly understand your audience.

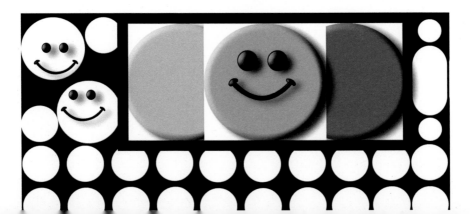

57.

THERE ARE BARRIERS TO EFFECTIVE COMMUNICATION

We all have barriers to effective communication, which vary in their importance to us. Taking these barriers into account will help you create strong and effective communications.

Here is a partial list of barriers, which I created after years of looking at human characteristics. These barriers are the main reason we have so many problems in the world. Collectively, they act as an enormous brake on creativity.

- Background
- Beliefs
- Culture
- Economic status
- Education
- Ethnicity
- Fears
- Gender
- Hatred

- History
- Intolerance
- Language
- Morals
- Nationalism
- Political status
- Prejudice
- Racism
- Religion
- Sophistication level
- Stereotypes
- Stigmas
- Temperament
- Tradition
- Tribe or affiliation
- Values

Because there are so many barriers to communication, each with their own weighting in our minds, the number of possible combinations runs into the billions. It's a daunting task to get around these barriers, and it can't be done without creative thinking.

Carefully consider each barrier to communication and design around it.

58.

SPEAK AND WRITE WITH CREATIVITY

You need to communicate well in order to apply new ideas. You need to express ideas so that your audience effectively receives, comprehends, and accepts them.

Whether you're speaking as a teacher trying to keep order in a classroom of 30 children or writing a proposal to convince your bank to finance your idea for your next billion-dollar product, the way you communicate will determine the success you have in implementing your ideas.

Have you ever said something that appeared to have been misunderstood by the person hearing it? Have you ever been offended by something you've read? Have you ever heard something described that hasn't made sense?

These are all examples of a communicator not applying creativity to reach the audience.

The next time you must communicate in any way—verbally, in writing, or visually—apply creative thinking before and during the creation of your communications. Use creativity as a tool to go beyond what you'd normally say or write or do, and you'll be more likely to successfully reach your intended audience.

Use creativity to communicate well.

PROBLEM SOLVING WITH CREATIVITY

59.

CREATIVITY CAN HELP YOU HANDLE DIFFICULT PEOPLE

Creativity is the best way to deal with negativity, whether it's being generated by you or someone you're interacting with. Creativity is what enables you to navigate and eliminate negativity.

Negative people are constrained in their outlooks. Their thinking is narrow and shaped by their own perceptions. They may lack empathy and compassion. They are both stressed and causing others to feel stressed.

Negative people see problems. When handed a bouquet of roses, they only see the thorns.

Creative thinkers are the opposite. They see solutions. They observe the unusual. They are tuned in to ingenuity. They are broad thinkers. They have ideas that no one else has.

Dissipate negativity with creative thinking.

60.

CREATIVITY REDUCES STRESS AND ANXIETY

I have made videos about people with dementia and depression. I've talked to a lot of people who've have had serious mental disorders.

People get stressed and depressed when they feel that they have few options. Some people commit suicide because they feel like they're totally out of options.

Creativity gives you options.

There may be instances in which a person can't see all their options broadly enough, but invariably, there is a myriad of solutions to every problem. A creative mind can always find options.

You can expand your thinking to use creativity to find those elusive options. The more creative you are, the more options you'll see. The more options you have as a human being, the less you'll feel stressed and anxious. The result is that you'll be more confident in confronting problems, making you a calmer person.

Creativity can help you
reduce stress.

61.

CREATIVITY IS FINDING NEW APPROACHES

Creativity can be applied everywhere, even at the fundamental level of tackling a problem or designing a product. There are many ways to approach problems, from applying different reasoning skills to methods of investigation to ways of searching for answers.

You can apply creativity when approaching a problem. Think differently about finding an alternate to your known solution approach.

Step back. Throw out your assumptions. Apply creativity at the very start of what you're trying to do. Explore every possible approach before you settle on one.

Apply creativity at the beginning of an approach.

62.

CREATIVITY LEADS TO THE UNKNOWN

Without creativity, inclusive analysis is stifled, often leading to the "known." "We know what the problems are; we just need to find the solutions" is a mantra of narrow-minded analysts. It usually means that the starting point is the wrong one.

Creativity leads to the unknown. It causes a widening of the known  to enable leaps of faith into exploring the unknown. It throws out assumptions, stereotypes, and givens, allowing a search for new truths.

Go where there are no "knowns."

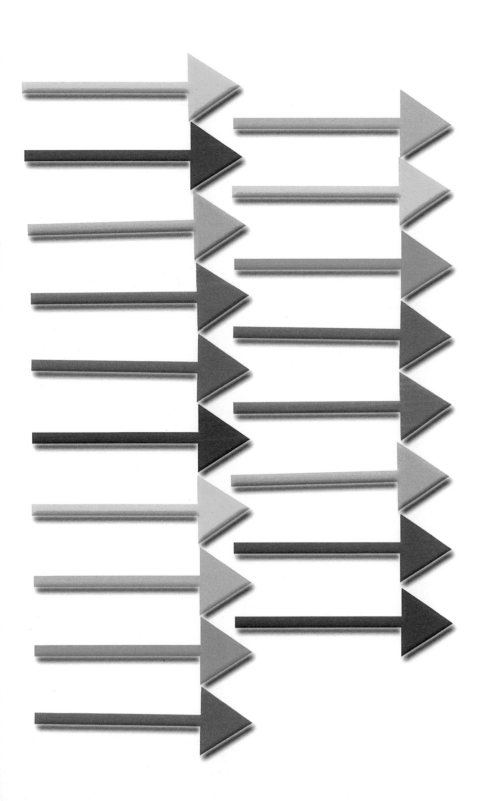

63.

CREATIVITY IS FINDING PROBLEMS

Can you identify and understand all the problems in your personal and professional life? I doubt it.

If you knew what your problems were, you'd set about solving them now. If we all did that, we would have fewer divorces and business failures.

In order to live a truly happy existence, we need to know what our problems are—all of them.

Creativity can help you identify problems, but you must be open-minded enough to proactively go looking for them.

Go out and actively find your problems.

64.

CREATIVITY IS SOLVING PROBLEMS

I wanted to create a global campaign in many languages to combat sexual and domestic violence. The immediate problem I saw was how to depict the characters in the series for a global audience. We all look different; have different skin, hair, and eye color; and wear different clothes.

After applying a lot of creativity, I came up with the solution you see in the image: blue animated characters with no hair, wearing simple clothes. Why blue and no hair? Because no one is blue and has no hair, so no one is excluded.

The series is called No Excuses, and the making of it was the subject of an hour-long documentary.

Once you find your problems, creativity can be hugely helpful in solving them.

Proactively seek the solutions to problems.

65.

CREATIVITY IS LOOKING AT EVERY ANGLE OF A SOLUTION

We all know people who think they have not only the right solution to a problem but also the only one.

You've seen ads in which the company or person selling products or services insists that their approach is the best way. "Follow my two steps and I'll make you insanely rich!" "Use this product and you'll never snore again!" "Buy our course and you'll be speaking fluent Finnish in six days!" The ads make it sound like the products, and they alone, have the answers.

Creativity is all about using multiple approaches. Use creative thinking to explore different approaches, methods, and ideas to problem solving. That means there are no such concepts as the only or best solution.

Creativity is a transformational thought process, so it can lead you to solutions to problems that defy obvious solutions. You don't reach an impasse in your mind when you're creatively thinking of solutions.

Explore all alternative solutions.

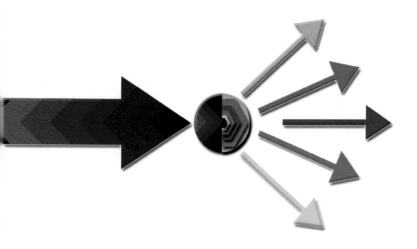

66.

CREATIVITY MAY LEAD TO MANY SOLUTIONS

Creativity could lead you to many different solutions to a problem. Indeed, if you apply creativity well, it should. There's a term for this: divergent thinking.

Multiple solutions are a good outcome. The best solution might be any of the possibilities or a blend of two or more.

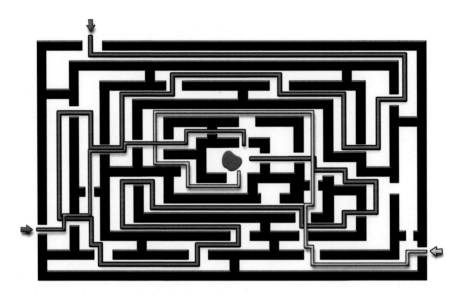

When confronted by a problem, allow your mind to wander freely. Don't stop thinking when you've thought of one possible solution. Write that one down but keep looking for others.

When you have a bunch of solutions, start to narrow them down until you have two or three. Then study each one intensively until you've decided on the solution that best solves your problem.

Think of many solutions to a
single problem.

67.

CREATIVITY PROMOTES FLEXIBILITY

Because creativity is the expansion of the mind, it fosters flexibility. This means you can start with part of a problem or project instead of the whole problem or project.

Any problem or project can be broken down into parts.

Think about designing a bicycle. You don't have to come up with the whole design right away. You can apply creativity to each component. You might start with the frame. And then you might stop because the design is so cool!

You might begin with the intention of redesigning the whole bicycle, but then see what your creativity produces partway through and decide that this is enough of a change. It makes the redesigning of the bicycle easier, faster, and cheaper because you don't have to think about how to change the handlebars and wheels.

Break apart any problem.

68.
CREATIVITY IS PROTOTYPING

What should animated characters look like for a global audience? The first solution I came up with in the No Excuses campaign was to have them wear no clothes. After all, they aren't people, so that could have worked, I figured. I had them drawn and then created in 3D animation, which is an expensive undertaking.

I was wrong. They looked nude! That would have turned people off. I had to think of another solution. I finally settled on very simple clothing that most people could wear. The clothes are universal and bland.

You might try many different solutions to a problem, as I did. It's a process called prototyping.

Prototyping is simply trying out an idea to create a product. It's an experiment. You actually create the product, but not in its final version. You might create a simple or cheap version of it.

If one prototype doesn't work, modify it or abandon it and try another. Keep trying different prototypes until one works perfectly.

Prototype your solutions to problems.

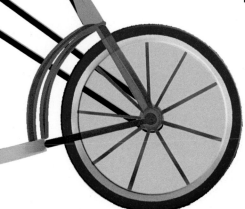

69.

CREATIVITY SOLVES THE MOST DIFFICULT PROBLEMS

This is The Three Amigos HIV/AIDS prevention program I directed and co-created.

Created at the height of the HIV/AIDS crisis in 2004–2005, the series has been widely credited with contributing to a slowing of the spread of HIV. It has been used in more than 150 countries. It has been produced in 45 languages, so more than 70 percent of the world's population can see the series in their own language.

Before this series, many attempts had been made to get people to use condoms to stop the spread the HIV/AIDS. Many campaigns were pulled off the air because they depicted real condoms and offended some people. Sex was making people sick. It was a difficult problem to tackle.

These three condoms were animation: they had faces and arms, and they talked. And they were very funny. They created in the viewer a suspension of their disbelief system. The viewer realized that what they were seeing was not real.

The series was played repeatedly in South Africa, which had the largest number of HIV-positive people, during a time of national angst. And then the three condoms took off around the world. We succeeded beyond our greatest hopes.

Think of a very complex or difficult problem you wish you could solve. Now tell yourself there is no problem for which there is no solution; you just haven't found the solution yet. Creativity will help you untie the tightest knots.

Creativity must be applied to the most difficult problems.

CREATIVITY AND YOU

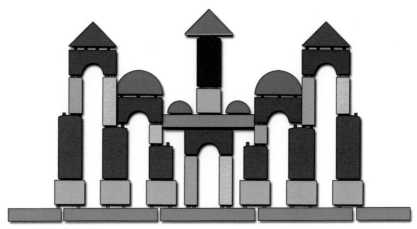

70.

YOU ARE CREATIVE

You are a creative being!

Think back to your childhood for the evidence. Did you:

- Stack blocks to construct your own castle?
- Sing, dance, draw, sculpt, act, or play an instrument?
- Make up your own rules for a game?
- Have an imagination you used continually?

Of course you did.

Accept that you are a creative person.

71.

WHY YOU MAY THINK YOU'RE NOT CREATIVE

Perhaps you think you're not creative. That may be because people are less creative as adults than they were as children. As most people grow older, their use of their imagination, in particular, diminishes.

Why? Because of our educational system. Of course, not all schools squeeze the creative juices out of children. However, many do. I was lucky to be able to attend an elite school that did not marginalize what I thought was important about myself.

I went to a private high school: The Cathedral and John Connon School in Bombay (as it was called then). It allowed for both creative and academic pursuits with very high standards. I acted and wrote plays and read poetry and debated.

I then went to a small public high school in Pennsylvania for an additional year as an exchange student. That school was populated by very dedicated teachers working with limited resources. The differences in teaching styles and standards required between these two high schools were gigantic.

Think about your school. Did it let you be who you wanted to be?

Be open to thinking like a child.

72.

REALLY, YOU ARE A CREATIVE PERSON

If you're still not convinced that you're already a creative person, I want you to do a little experiment.

Go and get a blank piece of paper, a pencil, and a string. That's all.

Put them in front of you. For the next 10 minutes, do whatever you want with those three objects. Anything you want. There are no rules, no expectations, and no right or wrong ways to use them.

Put the book down now and stop reading. Come back in 10 minutes.

Finished? Look at what you did. Whatever it was, it involved creativity.

You are a creative human!

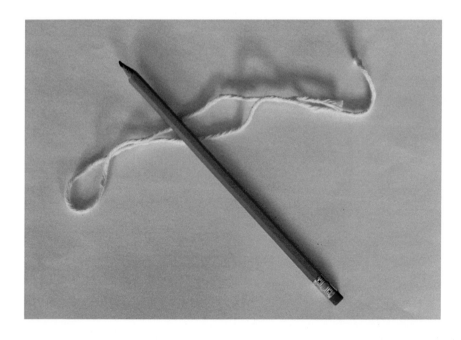

xvi

73.

PERHAPS YOU HAVE A BOX AROUND YOUR THINKING

This is Henry Ford, the founder of the Ford Motor Company. Here's a quotation attributed to him:

"If I had asked people what they wanted, they would have said faster horses."

He was right.

A non-creative person can think only "within a box." It's the creative person who can think outside the box. It's the very creative person, like Ford, who can think really far outside the box.

Be the really far outside-the-box thinker.

74.

USE CREATIVITY TO BREAK THROUGH CONSTRAINTS

We all feel constraints. We all feel that there are some things we simply cannot do. With creativity, you can expand where those constraints are.

I can't stand on one leg, even for a few seconds. You try it now. Time yourself. Go ahead—this book can wait.

It was longer than a few seconds, wasn't it? I'm jealous!

For the longest time, if I had to stand on one leg, I would hold my arms out to try to balance. Then I discovered that pressing my hands together in an Indian namaste helped me balance. I can now stand on one leg for at least three seconds!

Think of something you can't do very well. Now think of ways you might be able to do it better.

You can use
creativity to feel less
constrained.

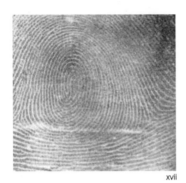

xvii

75.

YOU'RE UNIQUE

We are all individuals. No two human beings think and act in exactly the same way. Who you are changes the way you think and act. Just as you have unique fingerprints, you have a unique mindset.

That stands a lot of traditional marketing theory on its head. Until the age of the Internet, marketers grouped potential customers. They targeted products and services they thought I would want because they categorized me as an English-speaking, educated, urban man with sophisticated tastes.

Today, marketing is done on an individual basis. Gathering data on your very specific choices, likes and dislikes, and even your thinking has become big business.

Creativity is perfectly aligned with the new era of marketing. The more we exercise our creative thinking in the choices we make, the more we cannot be lumped together with others. Creative thinking is a highly individual process that leads to very tailored decisions.

There's only one of you.

94

76.

YOU DON'T NEED TO BE SUPER BRAINY

Creativity has a relationship to your personality; it does not have a relationship to your intelligence. This means you can be a perfectly average person in intelligence and still be a highly creative thinker.

It's your way of thinking that matters, not how intelligent you are or how much you know.

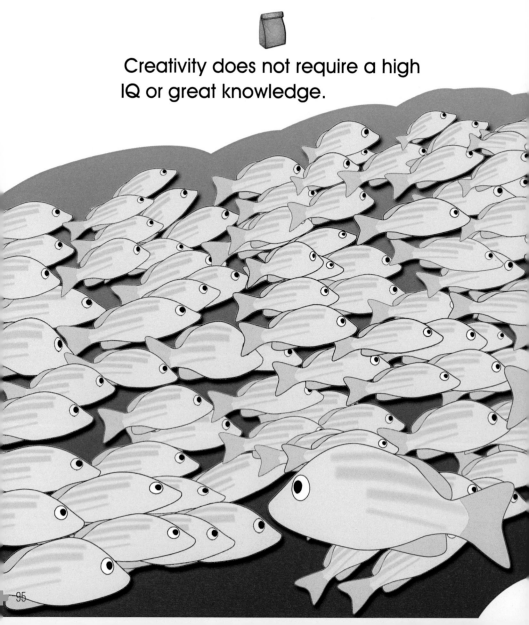

Creativity does not require a high IQ or great knowledge.

77.

YOU DON'T NEED TO BE PERFECT

Are you perfect? I doubt it. I have yet to meet a perfect human being. Are you universally loved? I have yet to meet a person whom everyone loves.

It's nice to want to be all things to all people. We all want to be liked, and there's nothing wrong with that. However, few of us come close to achieving it, and none of us actually do.

Perfection is definite: something is or is not perfect. Creativity is a multitude. You can be many things. You are this and that, good and bad, both at the same time.

Creativity is the antidote to perfection. It enables humans to be flawed. And that's what you and I are: flawed.

Creativity is your personalized ingredient for being an outstandingly imperfect human.

78.

YOU DON'T HAVE TO LOOK FAR FOR INSPIRATION

I received a commission from the Association of Migraine Disorders to create an animated video to encourage everyone to wear sunglasses in solidarity with migraine sufferers on the longest day of the year, June 21.

Looking around my office, I noticed the doorstop: a stuffed penguin. Yes! A penguin wearing sunglasses. What could be more appropriate?

**When you're looking for inspiration,
just look around.**

Here he is in 3D animation:

I named him Bob. He not only starred in the video but became the logo for the organization.

79.

YOU MUST CHANGE TO BROADEN YOUR CREATIVE THINKING

If you're a highly creative thinker, and this book merely confirms what you already know, congratulations. If you're not, what I'm calling for is nothing less than your opening up a whole new area of abilities and talents that may have been latent since childhood. Rediscovering your creativity will be an awakening.

We live in the most stimulating and fast-paced period in the history of humanity. Never before has an age seen such a surge of information, communication, and technology. This new age demands unprecedented capacities to cope and thrive.

It may be that you need to make only small, incremental changes; but it may mean you need to make huge leaps in your thinking, ingenuity, and creativeness. Only you can decide the degree of change you need, but embracing creativity almost certainly means you must change to some extent.

Embracing creativity means you will change.

xviii

80.

STEP OUTSIDE YOUR COMFORT ZONE

I got my first lesson in stepping out of my comfort zone for the benefit of others at the age of eight, when my mother took me to meet Mother Teresa in Calcutta, my hometown, several times.

Mother Teresa was not globally famous then. What I saw—numerous people who were very sick or dying—made a lasting and jarring impression on me. The image of Mother Teresa working in a huge room with the poorest of the poor dying on cots is still etched in my mind as if it were yesterday.

You can't just stay in the familiar, because if you do, you have no incentive to be creative.

You need to step outside your comfort zone to be creative.

81.

YOU CAN GO TO NEW PLACES

This is an image from a short animation I directed to address the stigma and long-term consequences felt by rape victims in Africa. It is called A Plea To My Father and was initially designed to be used in the Democratic Republic of the Congo.

I thought we should target the video to men. I was wrong. Women carried the video forward. They watched and used it. They first took it into neighboring countries. And then they shot it across the region to northeast Nigeria, where a murderous organization called Boko Haram had been kidnapping and raping high-school girls. Women there used it as a tool in classrooms to get girls to talk about rape.

With all my experience, I was not able to forecast the reach and impact of the video. That can happen when others see the results of your creativity.

Creativity can lead you to unexpected places.

YOU NEED CREATIVITY

82.

YOU NEED CREATIVITY IN YOUR PERSONAL RELATIONSHIPS

It doesn't matter who you are, you need creativity in your personal life.

Creativity can help you navigate the many ups and downs as you go through life. You'll feel more alive, curious, and connected with the world. You'll have a more aesthetic experience of life.

If you're not in a relationship, creativity could help you find love. You may find it by considering people who are outside the box of obvious candidates whom you usually date.

If you are in a relationship, creativity can help you find new ways to keep it fresh and lively. Successful couples say creativity is essential in a happy long-term relationship.

Stressed? Anxious? Life in the twenty-first century is fast-paced and competitive. Creativity can help you overcome stress and make you a better partner, parent, and friend.

There's a stress-management alternative to reaching for that tub of ice cream or sinking into a bubble bath or yodeling in the dark. You will find it by thinking creatively.

**You need creativity in your
personal life.**

83.

YOU NEED CREATIVITY IN YOUR WORK

No matter what field you're in, you need creativity in order to shine. Creativity leads to new ideas, insights, and methods. Creativity is a transformational power that helps individuals, companies, and organizations create new products and services that customers want.

To be an innovator and gain a competitive advantage, you need to fully develop your creative thinking skills, whether you work for yourself or for a company or an organization.

You need creativity to advance within your company or organization. You especially need it if you're stuck in a boring, go-nowhere job that you don't want to do!

You need creativity in your professional life.

84.

CREATIVITY IS THE SKILL THAT'S MOST IN DEMAND

What was the most in-demand "soft skill" in 2018, 2019, and 2020? In all three years, it was creativity. [xix]

If nothing else, the COVID-19 crisis showed us the critical need for creativity. Everything had to be re-thought, from how policy makers react to the pandemic to how businesses reach customers to how people continue to exercise while staying home.

Almost overnight, creative thinking came to the fore in every business, organization, and household. New processes had to be invented; new ways of thinking had to be found. Creativity became nothing less than a matter of survival. The year 2020 proved beyond a doubt that creativity is our most essential skill.

Creativity is the skill you need now.

85.

CREATIVITY IS THE TOP SKILL YOU NEED

As the world automates and artificial intelligence (AI) becomes omnipresent, creativity will distinguish us as human beings. Fortunately, robots can't think creatively, although they are getting closer to having that capability.

If you do something routine, from working on a production line to being a paper pusher, robotics or AI will soon be doing your job. Your job is toast. You're not a robot.

At the same time, technology has rapidly enabled all of us to widely express our creativity with everyone else. This revolution has changed our daily lives, from our ability to work from home and effectively communicate with colleagues and customers, to an explosion of creative content that is created, streamed, and watched by hundreds of millions of people via a myriad of platforms.

Technology is just one aspect of our rapidly changing world. So many challenges, from pandemics to climate change to social inclusion to economic and gender disparities, are thrusting change upon us.

We cannot run away from change. It has an impact on us, in small and large ways, every day.

Creativity can help you cope with change. Use it to see all your available options. Creativity is what you need to turn change from a problem into an opportunity.

Creativity is the most important skill to have in a changing world.

xx

86.

YOU CAN BE VERY CREATIVE IN DIFFERENT WAYS

Marie Curie won the Nobel Prize in physics and chemistry.

Leonardo da Vinci was (in alphabetical order) an anatomist, an architect, an astronomer, a botanist, a cartographer, an engineer, a geologist, an inventor, a mathematician, a musician, a painter, a palaeontologist, a scientist, a sculptor, and a writer.

John Forbes Nash Jr. was a mathematician and an economist. He is the only person to have won both the Abel Prize in mathematics (thought of as an equivalent to the Nobel Prize) and the Nobel Memorial Prize in Economic Sciences.

The fact that Curie, da Vinci, and Nash excelled in different subjects is not surprising. Creative thinkers apply their creativity to many different subjects and problems. When you open your mind to thinking creatively, you'll find all kinds of applications.

You can be highly creative in different areas.

WHAT YOU NEED IN ORDER TO EMBRACE CREATIVITY

87.

WHAT YOU SHOULD POSSESS AS A CREATIVE PERSON

You can be a creative person just for your own satisfaction.

What do you need if you want to go further in implementing creativity? You need the following eight elements, which are all related to each other.

You must have eight essential elements to implement creativity.

88.

YOU NEED A CREATIVITY-ENABLING ENVIRONMENT

You must have a conducive environment in which to be creative. This might be called an "organizational culture" in business or government. It might be the way you interact with those in your personal life.

Often, the people around you, in either your professional or personal life, create an unfavorable environment. The worst example of this is when someone summarily tells you that your idea cannot or should not be pursued. If someone's ever told you "That's the way it is" or "We've tried that" or "That can't be done," you know the person isn't creating the right environment.

I've come across many examples of environments that are not conducive to creative thinking. In 1995 I co-founded a media production company in Singapore. Even though I was there at the invitation of the government, which gave my partner, the brilliant Indian entrepreneur Ronnie Screwvala, and me lots of incentives, the environment wasn't right for a creative company because the country had not embraced creativity. There was a reliance on conformity.

Singapore's planners—and they truly are masters of planning—realized this. In the next two decades, the country transformed itself, and there is now a huge emphasis on creativity. Singapore has a thriving media industry and many leading-edge technology companies in which creativity is an essential ingredient. The environment has completely changed for creative thinkers.

Whether it's on a macro countrywide basis or just in your own small workplace, you must have an environment that facilitates creativity.

You must have a creativity-enabling environment.

89.

YOU NEED A FOCUS ON INNOVATION

If you work for an organization that highly values innovation, you're more likely to be a creative thinker. All the big tech companies, for example, know that they must highly value creativity, which results in innovation. Without it, they would die.

Motorola created the first mobile phone. For years, the company had a commanding presence in the mobile phone space, but it failed to see the importance of moving into smartphones and was soon overtaken by Apple, Samsung, and others. The people at Motorola used creativity brilliantly at the advent of mobile phones but failed to continue to apply it to create new innovations.

There are millions of Motorolas all over the world that have failed because of a lack of implementing creativity.

Creativity is what keeps organizations moving forward and able to compete in the marketplace. Creative thinking needs to be applied in every part of an organization, from the CEO to the lowest rank-and-file employee.

If you work in a place that lives by the mantra "It is what it is," you won't be able to be creative. Consider moving on.

You must have an emphasis on innovation.

xxi

90.

YOU NEED CREATIVE FREEDOM

Thinking creatively is all about having a free flow of ideas. Again, it doesn't matter if it is in your personal or professional life; you won't be able to be creative if you can't express yourself. You must have freedom.

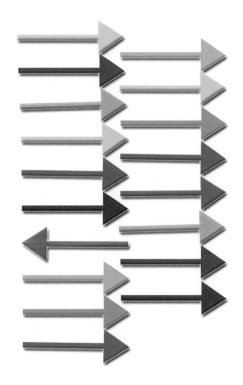

If someone laughs at you because you share an idea, no matter how stupid it may seem to them, they have a closed mind. Run away from that person. You wouldn't have expressed the idea if you hadn't thought it was worth articulating.

**You must be able to speak
openly with a free flow of ideas.**

91.

YOU NEED TO BE TREATED WITH RESPECT

History is replete with people who were told their ideas were dumb or unworkable and then went on to great success. Remember that for hundreds of years, even the most advanced thinkers thought the world is flat, and they laughed at, or persecuted, those who said the world is round.

That's not to say that all criticism should be rejected. Sometimes criticism can be very constructive and useful. However, it must be given, and received, in a receptive, open way. You need to be treated with respect.

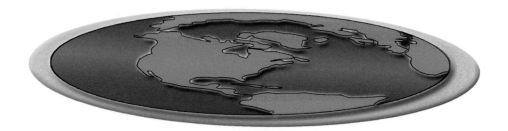

You must be listened to with respect.

92.

YOU MUST ASSUME MULTIPLE ROLES

In my work, I do everything from marketing to taking out the trash. For my films, I write the concepts, edit the scripts, direct the content production, supervise the voice recordings and music, and distribute the end products in multiple languages. That's a lot of hats to wear. Maybe that's why I have a collection of rather dashing hats!

It is very unusual for a creative person to wear only one hat. No entrepreneur, CEO, or leader of an organization wears just one, so they all need creativity.

You must take on multiple roles.

93.

YOU NEED SUPPORTIVE RELATIONSHIPS

No one is an island.

Thinking creatively is a solitary pursuit—something you do in your mind. That does not mean you can do anything concrete with your creativity by yourself. For instance, if you're an inventor with an idea for a new product, you may need someone to patent it, fund it, produce it, and market it.

If you're like most people, you want and need help from people such as a spouse, friends, business partners, and others.

Assess your personal and professional relationships. Consider whether you have enough of them. Perhaps you need new ones as you expand your mind to become more creative.

**Seek new relationships and
strengthen existing ones.**

94.

YOU NEED MONEY AND TOOLS

Even if you work for a highly innovative organization, you cannot do anything with a new idea unless you have money and tools. You need the ability to at least try out your creative ideas, if not fully realize them.

You can have the most brilliant idea, but if you don't have the means to implement it, it won't be of use to anyone.

You must have money and tools.

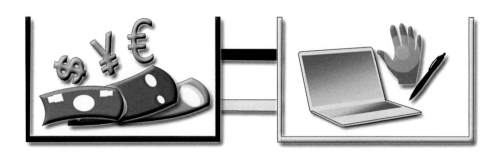

95.

YOU NEED ONE CHARACTERISTIC ABOVE ALL OTHERS

What is the one characteristic a creative person must have? Take a guess.

It's passion.

Passion is an essential element of creativity. You must intensely believe in yourself and your ideas.

I would have given up a long time ago if I didn't have passion for my creative work.

Passion is what drives me to this day. It's what motivated me to write this book to help you tune your mind toward creativity.

You must have passion.

MOVING FORWARD WITH CREATIVITY

96.

IT'S NEVER TOO LATE TO USE CREATIVITY

You might be thinking, "This is all good to know, but I'm set in my ways."

It doesn't matter how old you are; it's never too late to start using creativity. You can embrace it at any age or in any stage of your life.

There is no set age at which we reach peak performance or have the most fulfillment in life.

Studies have shown that as we go through life, from decade to decade, our abilities change but don't peak all at once: we get better at doing some things and worse at doing others. There is no age at which we are at the top of all aspects of our game.

**Embrace your creativity regardless of
your stage in life.**

97.

YOU CAN GET TO YOUR NEXT PEAK WITH CREATIVITY

People generally have multiple peaks and troughs in life, good times and bad, highs and lows. There is always a new peak waiting to happen. You can bring about that next high point in your life with a change in your thinking.

**Get to the next high in your life
with creativity.**

98.

MAKE A PROMISE TO YOURSELF

What's the promise you want to make to yourself? It's to reach immortality.

Immortality isn't becoming famous. It's not dedicating your life to some great achievement or endeavor. It's not changing the world. Not all of us can achieve those goals, and they're not what I'm suggesting.

Immortality is simply a single idea that outlives you. It is one way of doing, one concept, one process, or one product that doesn't die with you.

It's not that hard to achieve. If you apply your creativity, you'll come up with at least one idea that no one else has thought of. Just one is all you need.

That's immortality. That's what tuning your mind toward creativity could lead you to.

Reach for immortality.

99.

CREATIVITY IS WHAT YOU NEED TO REALLY SUCCEED

We all have different concepts of success. To achieve success, you must first define what success means to you.

Some people look at billionaires and think they embody success; others look at celebrities or leaders of countries. Many young people look at the number of followers on social media to gauge who's successful.

None of those are my definition of success. I have five "hopes" that form my definition of my personal success. I hope:

- I have lived the life I wanted to live by creating and traveling my own path.
- I have used all the talents that were given to me at birth to leave an imprint on the planet.
- I have loved as mightily as I could.
- I have given back as much as I could.
- Above all else, I hope that I am satisfied with who I am. Being satisfied means being true to myself and being at peace with my character.

Use your creative thinking to define your own success, and then use your creativity to work toward achieving that success. Nothing can be more important to you.

Creativity will lead you to success in life.

100.

THE BEST USE OF CREATIVITY: CREATING A REMARKABLE LIFE

You might use creativity to become a better partner, parent, communicator, engineer, bureaucrat, CEO, or taxi driver. Any of those would be good achievements. That's not the pinnacle of what you can achieve, however.

What's the single best thing you can do with your creativity? Use it to create your life.

No matter what stage you are at in your life or who you are with or what you do, you can use creativity to create a fantastic life from this moment on. Don't just live it. Don't drift with the flow. Don't let others decide it.

You can dream and design the life you truly want. Literally, proactively, and resolutely, create your life. This is your time. Go for it. Believe in you.

Create a remarkable life.

ACKNOWLEDGMENTS & INFORMATION

To my son and daughter

And to the thousands of family, friends, colleagues, and volunteers around the world who have joined me in a quest to better the human condition using mass communications over the last 25 years.

I am very grateful to several friends who read drafts of this book, especially Barbara, Caitlin, Heather, and Sarah who read multiple drafts.

Unless otherwise stated, all images are courtesy of Firdaus Kharas. Original graphics under the author's direction are by Narbu Chee. Copy editing is by Catherine Dee. Layout under the author's direction by Mirza Gohar Nayab.

Main website: www.chocmoose.com
Author's website: www.creativethinking.global
Vimeo channel for animations: https://vimeo.com/firdauskharas

The author is on Facebook, Twitter, and Instagram

A portion of the net profits from this book will be used to create and distribute life-saving behavior change communications in the poorest countries and communities.

Available as a hardcover, paperback, e-book and audiobook

Book ISBN: 978-1-7772422-0-6
Paperback ISBN: 978-1-7772422-3-7
E-book ISBN: 978-1-7772422-1-3
Audio book ISBN: 978-1-7772422-4-4

REFERENCES

i. 1982, Bell Telephone Magazine, volume 61, Number 1, "Creativity: It's the Thought that Counts," by Mary Ardito, page 32, published by American Telephone and Telegraph Company, New York

ii. My work can be assessed at https://vimeo.com/firdauskharas

iii. Image made by UPI photographer Arthur Sasse

iv. Joseph Karl Stieler/public domain

v. https://en.wikipedia.org/wiki/List_of_public_corporations_by_market_capitalization#2019

vi. By source (WP:NFCC#4), fair use, https://en.wikipedia.org/w/index.php?curid=49524231

vii. Image of Barker Shoes used with permission, can be found at https://www.barkershoes.com/

viii. By source (WP:NFCC#4), fair use, https://en.wikipedia.org/w/index.php?curid=52698540

ix. Wolfgang Amadeus Mozart/public domain

x. By Matthew Yohe, CC BY-SA 3.0, https://commons.wikimedia.org/w/index.php?curid=82773576

xi. "Steve Jobs Quotes." Quotes.net. STANDS4 LLC, 2020. Web. 9 May 2020, https://www.quotes.net/quote/45637

xii. By Leonardo da Vinci, www.vivoscuola.it: Home; picture, public domain, https://commons.wikimedia.org/w/index.php?curid=109273

xiii. Furnham, A. (2000), The Brainstorming Myth. Business Strategy Review, 11: 21-28. doi:10.1111/1467-8616.00154

xiv. By Studio Ellis & Walery:[1] Alfred Ellis (1854–1930)[2] & Walery (Stanislas Julian, Count Ostrorog, either senior (1830–1890) or junior (1863 - 1935).)[3] - Scanned from the 1914 edition of François Cellier & Cunningham Bridgeman's Gilbert and Sullivan and Their Operas, public domain, https://commons.wikimedia.org/w/index.php?curid=3987877 public domain, https://commons.wikimedia.org/w/index.php?curid=129583

xv. Jojhnjoy/public domain

xvi. By Hartsook, photographer. Image available from United States Library of Congress Prints and Photographs division under digital ID cph.3c11278 https://commons.wikimedia.org/w/index.php?curid=531177

xvii. Public domain

xviii. By Manfredo Ferrari, own work, CC BY-SA 4.0, https://commons.wikimedia.org/w/index.php?curid=35010569

xix. https://business.linkedin.com/talent-solutions/blog/trends-and-research/2020/most-in-demand-hard-and-soft-skills

xx. Henri Manuel/public domain

xxi. Public domain